Table of contents

Acknowledgements

About the author

Introduction

Two

A rainy day

Ambitions

People

School dinners

Snowflakes

Feelings

My strange dream

Books

Shadows in my mind

Colours of autumn

My paint box

Daffodils

Autumn

A spring poem

Winter is here

Language week

A prayer

Acknowledgements

I would firstly like to thank God who makes all things possible and is more than worthy of all praise. I would like to thank my mother Jacqueline for her support throughout my life. I want to also thank my younger sister, Vivian for assisting me with the typing of this book. Horace Cole and Kadian Bailey also get my gratitude for assisting with the first typed draft of these poems. Finally I want to thank Samuel Thompson for assisting me to proofread and giving his kind comments and encouragement.

About the author

I was born in St. Catherine, Jamaica and was introduced to reading and developed a love for it at an early age. I also started writing when quite young. I grew with my mother and younger sister and graduated from the St. Catherine High School, St. Jago High School and Northern Caribbean University. I am a firm believer in God and also enjoy sports, browsing the internet, music and television.

Introduction

These poems were written when I was between the ages of about nine to eleven years old. They mainly target and I believe are best suited for children of a similar age group and early teens. I do however believe that they can and will be enjoyed by persons of various backgrounds and ages. Enjoy reading!

Two

Two little birds up in the sky,
Two little butterflies fluttering by,
Two little fish in a pool so deep,
Two little children fast asleep.

A rainy day

It is a rainy day
No-one is out to play,
The sky is very grey,

I will not go out today.

The umbrellas are out everywhere,
Big puddles here and there,
We walk streets with care,
Because umbrellas are in galore there.

A rainy day a rainy day,
When we walk with care,
Because if we slip,
We might break a bone on a stone.

Ambitions

Ambitions, ambitions, pure ambitions,
Some people have strong ambitions,
Some people have lots of ambitions,
Some people have fun ambitions.

Some people have no ambitions,
Some people have low ambitions,
Some people have few ambitions,
Ambitions, ambitions, pure ambitions.

People

The world is full of people,
People doing their jobs,
some people simply rob,
some people are called Bob.

Some people keep frogs,
Some people like logs,
Some people like to play with hogs,

Some people like to play in fog.

Some people like to watch slugs,
Some people like to sit down on rugs,
Some people like to hug,
Some people like it when they feel snug.

Some people, some people,
There are all different kinds of people.

School dinners

Sometimes school dinners are nice,
Sometimes the potatoes are fossilized,
Sometimes the rice is dry,
And it is cold just like ice.

When there is rice on the ground,
Some of the children have to brush it up,
Or soon there will be mice,
Eating up all the rice.

Snowflakes

Snowflakes,
Some lakes of snowflakes,
I need to tie my lace so that snowflakes do not get in my shoe.

When I step in snowflakes I leave a trace,
A naked trace of snowflakes.

Feelings

People have sad feelings,
Happy feelings,
Courageous feelings and humorous feelings,
And other feelings.

If you say something bad to someone,
They have upset feelings,
Feelings are emotions.
If you say something nice to someone they feel good,

If you say something funny to someone they have humorous feelings.

Feelings change in every different situation,
If someone gets into an argument,
They feel angry at the other person who they are arguing with.

Feelings can be strong,
Feelings can be weak,
We all have feelings.

My strange dream

I had a strange dream,
I was not a human being,
I was as big as a cinema screen,

The people were so scared,
Because I was the most feared,
They ran as I neared,
Because I was the most feared.

Books

Have you read the book of 'Krindlekrax',
Thundering down the street?
Have you read the book of 'Matilda'?
She liked to read.

Have you read 'The BFG'?
He had big feet,
I think that some books are great
And I give them a very high star rate

And when you read some books
Straight away they catch you on their liking bait.

Shadows in my mind

Shadows in my mind,
Shadows in my mind,
That shadowy figure is always close behind,
Following me everywhere I go.

When I run fast and when I walk slow,
When I am on the train
And when I am at home,
Those shadows in my mind are always there.

Colours of autumn

The autumn grass is green,
It is a beautiful scene,
The sun is bright yellow,

The sky is blue.

The dried up leaves that have fallen off the trees are yellow
And some are brown,
All falling off the trees onto the ground.

Butterflies are black and red,
Landing on the flowers,
They flap their wings
And off they go again.

It is nice to sit down in the park
And look at the fresh green grass
And the leaves on the ground,
There are so many beautiful butterflies,
So many big brown trees,
With so many yellow leaves.

There are lots of children in the park
And lots of dogs running around fast,
Playing with balls and racing each other.

People are buying their winter clothes
Because when it is autumn,
Everyone knows that winter is near.

My paint box

Orange is the colour of the sun,
Green is the colour of the grass,
Blue is the colour of the happiness,
Shared by everyone.

Black is the colour of midnight,
Brown is the colour of the foxes,
Running around early in the morning.

Grey is the outline of the rocky mountains,
Transparent is the clear water,
Flowing down the waterfalls.

Purple is the colour of the butterflies,

Flying around in the air,
My paint box is filled with many different colours.

Daffodils

Daffodils, daffodils everywhere,
Daffodils, daffodils, floating in the air,
Oh daffodils aren't they beautiful in the sunlight?

Daffodils are so nice, That this morning I picked some
And put them in my mother's flower vase
And oh my mother adored them
And she said
"Daffodils, daffodils, aren't they beautiful"?

Autumn

Here comes autumn season,
With the harvest time,
Animals hibernating,
For the winter time.

Leaves change colour,

Red, gold and brown,
Fresh autumn breeze,
Brings the leaves down.

Ripe, juicy apples,
Crispy, crunchy corn,
Green pears and grapes,
Cucumber and lettuce on my plate.

Rich golden harvest is gathered,
All in autumn,
It is a busy time for the farmers,
From early in the morning.

A spring poem

Spring is coming,
The sun is shining very brightly,
Everyone is happy,
Because spring is near,
There is no gale,
And the sky is clear.

The air is fresh,

I like the smell of fresh air,

With the scent of flowers mixed in the air.

Winter is here

Winter is here

And people are playing in the snow,

Having snow fights,
Or making snowmen,
We are having lots of fun,
The snow is very cold,
But we do not mind.

You have to be careful when you walk,
The snow is very slippery,
It is all over the roads,
Some vehicles are slipping off the roads.

Winter is cold,
Winter is snowy,
But whether you like it or not,
We all have to face the fact,
That winter is here.

Language Week

Language week is a week of fun,
It is fun for everyone,
You should join in and show the work you have done,
You should invite your family too.

Tell them to come along and enjoy themselves,
They can join in too,
I am sure that when the week is over,
You will be bursting with joy,
So whatever you do please remember,
Language week is here.

The whole school has worked so hard,
To prove that they can do very good work,
Stories, poems and lots more,
It's going to be a language galore.

A prayer

Oh Lord,

As it is the end of the day,

I am going to rest,

Because I want to wake up happy tomorrow.

Bless me today and forever-more,

In Jesus name I pray,

Amen.

THE END

www.ingramcontent.com/pod-product-compliance
Lightning Source LLC
Chambersburg PA
CBHW041745040426
42444CB00001B/40